Cultivating Essence
From the Matrix of Soul

*Sustainable Systems
for a Flourishing Humanity*

Awaken the World Within

Find Your Forward Flow

Embrace a New Vision

Dawn Richerson

Cultivating Essence from the Matrix of Soul
Sustainable Systems for a Flourishing Humanity

© 2012, 2025 Dawn Richerson

Lifeseeds Press is an imprint of
Soul Simple Innovation LLC

ISBN 978-0-9887947-7-1 hardcover
ISBN 978-0-9887947-8-8 paperback
ISBN 978-0-9827692-9-4 e-book

This book may not be reproduced in whole or in part, without written permission from the publisher, except by a reviewer who may quote brief passages in a review. Nor may any part of this book be reproduced, stored in a retrieval system, or transmitted in any form or by any means—electronic, mechanical, photocopying, recording, scanning, or otherwise.

Library of Congress Control Number 2015914064

Learn more about the author and her work:

- soul-simple.com
- dawnricherson.com

FOR ALL THE
GENERATIONS

8 SACRED MOVEMENTS TO CULTIVATE YOUR ESSENCE
& FOSTER SUSTAINABLE SYSTEMS FOR A FLOURISHING HUMANITY

1. **Begin with an inside-out approach** and cultivate you. Start with core connection.

2. **See the hidden wholeness** in all things and make the journey back to sacred wholeness, including and honoring all inner voices and perspectives, welcoming all to the banquet table.

3. **Experience the winds of grace** and celebrate the unfolding mystery of life. Trust in the unfolding process and the revelation of the whole of who you are.

4. **Give generously from the heart** and share from the streams of your soul, taking care to replenish and nourish your being.

5. **Honor the creator within** and tap your inner guidance system, trusting who you truly are, honoring others, and acknowledging the goodness of life.

6. **Show up fully here and now** and find the courage to fully participate in your life and in your world. Enter this moment of now and receive fully the gift of the present by being present to its wonder.

7. **Engage in dialogue** and celebrate diversity within unity. Begin with inner dialogue and essential conversations through natural networks of support.

8. **Learn to be in community** and celebrate the connections being revealed among us in every moment. Become comfortable with who you are and celebrate your contribution to the whole.

CONTENTS

The Story of Beginnings 7
Eternal Lights Shining in the Darkness 8
Separating Light from Darkness 10
The Life Within Lights Our Way 12
The Key to Interconnectivity Is Inner Connectivity 14
Waking Up 15
Learning to Sing Again 16
Lullaby 17
There Is No Harmony Without Resonant Consonance 18
The Wonder of Seeing through New Eyes 19
Seeds of Recognition 20
Allow What Is to Be 21
Choosing Now 22
Where's Your Sense of Humor? 23
Look Up! 24
This is Your Message in a Bottle 25
Discombobulated by Direction 26
Up in Smoke 27
Ashes to Ashes 28
Grace Unfurls Its Wings 29
Life is the Cradle 30
The Infinite Now 31
All in All 32
Markers 33
Weather 34
Down Came the Rain 35
No Compromise 36
Beauty unto Beauty 37
Trail Mix 38

Belonging	39
Trajectory	40
Shooting Stars	41
The Home Stretch	42
Double Dares and Life on the Leading Edge	43
Forever and This Day	44
Telling Truth in a Tone-Deaf World	45
The Speed of Light	46
Forgiving	47
Origin and Originality	48
The Dream We Dreamed	51
Reaching for Rivers of Hope	52
Ebb and Flow	54
Staying Current	55
Distillation	56
Maybe You're Just Rusty	57
Breath	58
Born Free	59
Retrieval	60
Flix	61
Flex	62
Flux	63
The Moving Spiral Staircase	64
Curve Speed	65
A Cup of Coffee	66
Traffic	67
Reclamation	68
Breaking Bread	69
Get in the Story	70
Fault Lines	71
Cooperation	72
Surprise!	73

Open the Present, Already	74
Compensation	75
Let Me Hear Your Body Talk	76
Out of the Hive and into the Cuckoo's Nest	77
Aphids and Aphrodite	78
Matriculation	79
Cycles of Work and Play	80
Seeking Something	81
The Context of Community	82
The Music of Solitude	83
Stop Waiting for the Answer	87
Unlimited Direction	88
Search and Rescue	89
Time Passages	90
Parallels in Space and Time	91
Unveiled	92
Interior Design	93
Adornment	94
Changing Clothes	95
Leaving Limitation Behind	96
Snack Time	97
Form and Function	98
Become a Connoisseur of Change	99
Never Miss an Opportunity to Choose	100
Stand Your Ground	101
Free Spirit	102
Intrepid Souls in Transit	104
Pirates!	105
Goodbyes	106
P.S.	107

Note from the Author

THIS BOOK IS A LOVE NOTE TO THE WORLD. It is informed by my firm conviction that all things are connected and that we are loved beyond measure. I cannot claim the ideas you will read here as my own original design. I was merely the conduit for this message, opening my heart and soul to allow the gift of this new vision for our world to break through, first in the mysterious though undeniable form of love and grace and then with words on the page.

My soul desire is that the fresh winds of hope for humanity that come to life in this message stir your soul as they did mine. There is no question that the winds of change are blowing in our world. My belief is that they are winds of grace—the sweet whisper of a dream breathed into the possibility for a flourishing humanity.

Feel those winds. Imagine the dream alive.

The ideas set forth in the pages that follow were a gift of grace in my own life. They seemed to be planted in me. The conduit for my awakening to these seeds for life was my own heart and soul. The words were given to me. I first began to share them publicly in November of 2011, twelve years after I they sprung to life within me. They came quickly, a sudden tumble of grace and an infusion of timeless truths that I am still absorbing.

Initially, I saw the sole source of this material as a beloved mentor who died too soon. I now see that the message itself was embedded in the sacred seeds of essence I myself had come bearing and were from the very source of Source of life that lived in me. *Cultivating Essence* is for any and for all who want to walk with grace through this messy life. It is for those who long to know why they are here now and live into that truth more fully. There are always two roads. We are given a choice. Two roads diverged, and two roads will converge again one day.

Which will we choose?

Less-traveled paths are rough and rocky. Some choose it for that appeal. Others see the wide, well-worn path and choose the easy road. We can climb the rigorous mountains. Or we can even be transported, effortlessly I am told, from one view of reality to another. Either way, we will arrive where we began. Either way, the journey will be beautiful. I have been blessed on my journey. I have been loved despite my every attempt to thwart life's love for me.

And still it pursues me. It envelops me. It changes me.

I invite you into the dance of your life. It is my hope that these core passages and the soul-activating energy that runs through them and beneath them awaken you to your whole self and your soul self. Allow yourself to surrender just long enough to catch a glimpse of all that is most beautiful within you and around you, to cultivate essence and to breathe deeply from the matrix of soul from which we come and go.

Know now that you are held in an infinite grace, treasured and beloved from beyond and from within.

With an ever-widening love for God, who is our home,

CULTIVATING ESSENCE FROM THE MATRIX OF SOUL

For a Flourishing Humanity

THE FOUNDATION OF ALL LIVING THINGS IS LIGHT, and it is love that sustains all life. You and I and all living things are designed as sustainable systems within ourselves. We are meant to live, meaning we are here to experience life in all its fullness. This is the motivation and purpose for sharing these ideas for life.

The whole creation is brought to life as a full expression of love in its infinite variety. Life itself is dynamic and ever changing. We are always growing, pulled toward greater expression. As Dylan Thomas put it, "The force that through the green fuse drives the flower, drives my green age."

This is our green age. It is not just the individual who is meant to flourish, but the whole of humanity and all living systems. If we are to thrive and not just survive, we must return to those things which sustain life and support our full flourishing. We must release all false structures and systems, recreating our lives and our world with life-giving systems.

But before we move too quickly to systems design, we must fully immerse ourselves in a new kind of knowing that honors what was forgotten through the saga of human history. We must remember the seeds for life that were hidden in plain sight, reflected in the natural world and embedded in the very fabric of who we are.

First, we awaken the world within for a whole new way of seeing who we are. Then, in our individual lives and in communities of belonging, we find our forward flow. We discover a whole new way of being and begin to move through life more naturally, unbound by all that would tell us we are anything less than loved fully as we are.

Awake to life and moving with it, rather than fighting to conquer it, we begin to embrace a new vision for who we are, individually and collectively. We reinvent our lives and engage in course correction. We find a whole new way of freeing ourselves and all is lifted up.

Free at last and reconciled to life, we walk in the way of wholeness, moving into a new era, rich in love. Never again will we forget that at our core we are, as all living things are, composed of light and love. Never again will we question the inherent goodness of life.

This is our Great Return. It is a remembrance.
It is the revelation of life's mystery.

Its time is now. This is the time we stand together and unfurl again a banner of love, allowing that love to fuel the dynamic and sustainable system that we are.

This book is a manual for the many, a "message in a bottle for the world." I am merely a vessel, a messenger. Rather than instructional guide, the message of *Cultivating Essence from the Matrix of Soul* is an array of blinking starlight offered in celebration of the journey we are making. It is infused with love for the whole of humanity and for each unique expression of the one love that sustains all life.

The ninety seeds for life support you in coming fully to your LIFE so that you might Live In Full Expression, following your unique patterns of life and bringing forth a creation of love to offer back to life and the giver of life. The seed ideas for life work together as a map for your full thriving. Unlike most maps, the message itself is a living one. It may be accessed in unique ways and is brought to life by each one of us uniquely as we come and go.

My hope for this book is that it reconnects you with the light, life, and love you are at your core and encourages you to live fully from a newfound celebration of who you are. What matters most now is that your joy and mine are made complete through full thriving in each day.

I dream of a new world, a world where we each bring forward a particular play of light, celebrate and share our essential story of life, and usher in together a revolution of love. The sustainable systems for flourishing humanity we will bring forward will be born from our ability and willingness to draw deeply from the endless pools of soul within.

For a flourishing humanity...

This is why we are making this journey. That all might know themselves as light, life, and love, one with the whole creation. Is this not a better meaning to choose for our lives—that you and I, imperfect as we are, might come to LIFE and Live In Full Expression one magical moment at a time?

There is a story of life alive inside of you.

As you tap and share its wisdom, you contribute something of inestimable value to a flourishing humanity. Never doubt wild magnificence and wonder of your soul singing its singular song.

Introduction

HERE ON EARTH, WE MOVE AS TILLERS OF A NEW ERA, rich in love. Rooted in the magical and the miraculous, we are growing back toward the ground of God. We are planted in this world not by accident. We are here by choice. Each and every one of us.

We were chosen. And we chose.

We come carrying seeds of essence, particular expressions of the infinite Divine meant to be scattered in the fertile atmosphere of this place and time. These seeds of promise within each one of us hold the potential for a new world not constricted by the belt of reason, circumstance, or traditional belief, but rather expanded wholly by the gift of who we are. I see us connected one to the other and lifted in thanksgiving for this opportunity to return to the wholeness of who we once were and who we are even now.

Whether we make this journey will be determined by the choices we make on a daily basis, moment by moment. The roads we choose to follow every day lead us either in the direction of fulfilling the call to which we once said, "Yes." Or they take us farther away. Are we traveling in the way that leads us home?

We come to this world as little babies, eyes closed, curled up, tiny toes wiggling as we become accustomed to the feeling of our bodies. Innocent and pure, each one of us carries something vital and precious. Some of us know this from the beginning. Others have forgotten.

How we use the gifts that we are given—the gift of who we are—is up to us. We have been given free will, and the choice of whether we use all of who we are and how we do so is ours alone. It's up to each one of us. Whether we acknowledge it, whether we choose to nurture it, whether we keep it to ourselves or whether we throw open the whole our life and loose it to the wind—these decisions will determine our common course.

This world affords us many opportunities to cover up the truth, to smother the seed and squander its gift. At every turn, we may be tempted to hide from the light we bear. It's easy to get lost. It's easy to convince ourselves we have nothing of value to share. The question of *"Who am I?"* rattles around in our mind. It's easy to set what we know we are here to do aside for a later time—when we know more, when we have achieved some measure of success, when we feel ready or brave or healed.

Now is the only time.

Now, in our time, we must become like gardeners, nurturing and nourishing what we carry in these bodies, tending to it daily and allowing it to grow to its fullness. It is our responsibility and ours alone to choose to honor the unique sacred gift within us and to breathe life into that tender gift of mercy. We must become a community of gardeners, learning from those among us who have quietly been living in this way among us.

We must intentionally clear out the weeds within and prune overgrown branches. It is up to each one of us to ensure that that seed within receives the space, sustenance and sunlight it needs to grow, that it is protected from the storm so that it can take root. We must tend to the seeds of grace with patience for life's unfolding process and water them with our love.

Only then will those precious gifts be seen and received by those who will recognize within us the message they most need to receive. Only then can we water the world.

This is the moment of the Great Turning.

If we turn back to the care of our souls, we may yet find redemption and grace unimagined. If we lose our footing, we may fall back into forgetfulness and, for a time, that sacred seed planted within might be lost to others.

The stakes are high. The time is ripe. The world is waiting.

We are the creators of a new society—an internal agrarian society that will lead to a civilization far more humane than that which we have created to date as we focused on building external systems, organizations, and structures.

Start with everything you already have.

Tend to it. Care for that which has been entrusted to you. Bring it into harmony with all that is. Riff on its singular magnificence and allow that to awaken our world and all those who have come bearing their own song to amazing possibility.

We are only at the beginning, after all.

Let's go!

The Story of Beginnings

EACH OF THE WORLD'S THREE monotheistic religious traditions shares the concept of light emerging from darkness. *In the beginning: light. Light called forth. Light drawing us toward it. Light within. Light not fully understood. Light bursting forth and shining through.*

> **In the beginning God created the heavens and the earth.** Now the earth was formless and empty, darkness was over the surface of the deep, and the Spirit of God was hovering over the waters. And God said, "Let there be light," and there was light. God saw that the light was good, and he separated the light from darkness.
>
> ~ from the Judeo-Christian tradition, Genesis 1:1-2,
>   *The Torah*

> **Allah is the Light of the heavens and the earth.** The Parable of His Light is as if there were a Niche and within it a Lamp: the Lamp enclosed in Glass: the glass as it were a brilliant star: Lit from a blessed Tree, an Olive, neither of the east nor of the west, whose oil is well-nigh luminous, though fire scarce touched it: Light upon Light! Allah doth guide whom He will to His Light: Allah doth set forth Parables for men: and Allah doth know all things.
>
> ~ from the Islamic tradition, Surah 24. An-Nur (Light), 35,
>   *The Koran*, (Yusuf Ali Translation)

> **In the beginning was the Word, and the Word** was with God, and the Word was God. He was with God in the beginning. Through him all things were made, without him nothing was made that had been made. In him was life, and that life was the light of men. The light shines in the darkness, but the darkness has not understood it.
>
> ~ from the Christian tradition, John 1:1-5,
>   *The Bible* (New International Version)

Eternal Lights Shining in the Darkness

Our world has never needed light more. Our lives have never needed light more. Yet, the busy pace of our lives and the rapid evolution of new technologies in our time have, for all their improvements, only exposed the fact that what is merely external can never illuminate that which lies inside the human heart.

While the continued unfolding of new technology and the exploration of the external is important work, we stand on the precipice of an awakening that begins within. Now, it is time to explore the interior truths that can only emerge when we, individually and collectively, embrace the light shining in the darkness within our hearts.

We have been afraid to go too deep, afraid of what might lurk within the recesses of our hearts and minds.

We know too well the wounds of this world. Even those of us who have embraced healing and invested significant resources in cleaning up thoughts, emotions and behaviors have held onto an outdated belief that this is work, and hard work at that.

Some of us have become experts at roaming around in the darkness within. Courageously, a few among us have dared to open the vast unknown within to a source of light we have perceived to be outside ourselves, perhaps from some far-off deity or from the enlightenment of more evolved souls who have journeyed with us through this world. We have been reaching for a solution that comes from outside ourselves.

The truth is that we have all the light we need. We carry it within. Nothing external is needed.

What *is* needed is an awakening to the worlds within.

In this time of great change, humanity faces a choice. Will we awaken to the truth that we are eternal lights shining in darkness? Or will we continue to scramble in some last-ditch effort to fix the darkness we see as closing in? Will we choose illumination or will we remain entrenched in the illusion of separation?

Separating Light from Darkness

BEFORE ANY OF US CAN HOPE TO BRING FORTH the light within, or even see through the darkness to which we have grown accustomed, we must release the old beliefs about ourselves to which we cling in desperation.

We have long believed ourselves to be a people immersed in the shadow of this world, wanderers through a cold, dark night or vagabonds blinded by the desert's stinging sun and sand.

Make room for a new story, the creation of a wondrous wave upon whose crest rides the hope of humanity.

Even now, in this time, the beating of a million hearts cry out with a longing to rush toward the shores of a new understanding of who we are as beings of light. We long to know our light, thanks in large part to those pioneering souls among us who have called us, again and again, back to this truth.

Awakening to the light within begins by acknowledging the darkness we have known so well and then separating that darkness out to allow the Light to emerge.

What darkness have we known?

Separation within. Separation without. Division within. Division without. Chaos within. Chaos without. Addiction. Brokenness. Disease. War. Alienation. Poverty. Inequality. Subjugation. Devastation and deconstruction. Waste.

What am I forgetting?

Having identified and called out the darkness we know, it is time to see what does not belong to the darkness and to give it equal consideration:

Faith, flowing where there seems to be no evidence or cause.
Hope, springing up in the most unlikely of circumstances.
Love, mirrored in the lives we encounter every day.

Once we begin to see the light all around us, breaking forth through any darkness, we are ready to trace it back to the seed from which it grew. How did this light find its way out into our world? What was the source of the faith, hope and love we have known?

And how is this light, born of ordinary people from all walks of life, a reflection of the one light within you?

Where in you can you separate out light and call it good?

The Life Within Lights Our Way

IN EVERY MOMENT THERE IS a point of choice.

Will we move ever upward and expand outward along the ever-widening spiral of our lives? Or will we contract and, slipping down, revert to a sort of sleeping sickness?

Or, perhaps more damning, will we succumb to the illusion that there is no choice at all and simply pass through this life and this world in a sort of perpetual spin cycle?

We choose the meaning we attach to the events of our lives and that choice sets us in motion in one direction or another.

It is never about what happens. It is always about what we tell ourselves about what happens. More accurately, it is about the story we tell ourselves about who we are. It only means what meaning we choose to assign. This is a difficult truth to grasp.

We have passed the time of excuses. You alone sculpt your reality. You alone shape the future you will experience.

You are now responsible for everything that happens in your inner environment. What happens around you is simply a reflection of what collectively you have allowed to be planted in the sacred garden of your hearts and souls. If you want a good gauge of how you are doing, take a look around.

But this is not to say that all is lost.

You may go back now and reshape your reality by choosing a new interpretation, by seeing what you have believed is only one possible version of the truth. Experiment by choosing a meaning that also allows you to stand fully in your power as the creator of your life and that allows others to be in harmony with the whole of who they are and their expression of their true selves at any given point in time.

Release the need for perfection and embrace wholeness. Then you will uncover the unfathomable uniqueness of who you truly are.

The Key to Interconnectivity Is Inner Connectivity

BEGIN AT YOUR CORE. See the beautiful lines that connect one facet of who you are to the other. Discover the seeds that are hidden in plain sight within your heart. We open up, fullness into fullness, from the tiniest seed of infinite possibility.

And it is such a fragile process.

We hurt when that tiny seed is pricked by life.

Sometimes we hurt so much we curse the seed and deny the very essence of who we are. To do so is to ignore the very thing that would set us free. We are meant to live from the wholeness of who we are, to connect to that first and then to each other. Connect deeply and often to your still center.

God is there. You are there.

Waking Up

W<small>E ARE TRAVELERS ON</small> a common journey.

The first step to the next step on that journey is for each of us, beginning in this moment, to clear limiting beliefs we have formed because others could not acknowledge the truth of their own souls and, as such, could not have dared to see us for who we truly are.

The next step to the next step is to see our way back to the beauty of who we are and to celebrate that. Wildly.

There are easier ways to wake up than for your entire body to reverberate to the sound of a harsh doorbell at six o'clock in the morning. Yet, this is the situation you now find yourselves in. Listen to the gentle hum of your life. Almost imperceptible at first, it will stir you back into the opportunity of the moment.

In the stillness there is a song that will rise up within you.

And it is unlike the song of any other. It is yours alone to sing, and in the singing you will remember.

And as you remember more of who you have always been, your song will carry on the wind. And more will be awakened to their own melodies. And soon the universe will harmonize to the beauty of your voice and your hearts will become an unstoppable chorus of change.

Learning to Sing Again

YOU HAVE LEARNED IN THIS LIFE to curl up with your treasures, to cradle yourselves against those who might label you as "other than," to safely tuck away the truth of who you are in an effort to guard yourself from attack.

But your song is not meant only for you. The song of your soul is but one strain of a universal symphony.

Some of you treasure your gift but only for yourselves. Others of you are frightened by the very sacred seed that lies within you, and so you bury it deeper and cover it with busy-ness, with mindless activity, addiction and distraction. Over time, you fall into a deep sleep and the world is robbed of who you are. And you are lost to your pseudo-selves, selves which fragment the one whole truth of who you are.

You must embrace the whole of who you are, but the embrace is not enough. You must share your soul self and watch the gift be multiplied. Find the fortitude and courage to step out onto the waves and know who you are is all you need.

Sing out in faith and listen for the wind's reply.

Some of you convince yourselves that the song is only an imagining, wishful thinking, or a futile longing for what can be no more. You are frightened by what wells up within you. You do not understand it. You do not want it. Some of you want only to experience this physical realm in which your soul is housed and so set off on an arduous, careful journey to cover up what is within you. But the cost of doing so is steep.

If you are to awaken the world, you must sing again the song of yourself.

Lullaby

WE START AT THE BEGINNING, with the infant that comes to this world innocent. Knowing. Pure. And wise. And we imagine that infant inside of us. With a gentle compassion, we reach within and cradle that infant in our arms.

And we simply begin to hum.
And then to sing.

A lullaby. An anthem. The magical mystery tour begins.

Trust yourself to know the tune and to sing the child in you awake. Ah, to see her whole and complete, her heart beating with the force of life. Each breath she takes a reconnection to the Divine from which she came. And as her eyes open, gaze down upon her with deep love and honor. Know she has come to be your teacher.

From this moment on, assure her that you will care for her. And as you realize she is gazing back upon your face, imagine what it is she wants you to know right now.

Hear her.
See her.
Love her.
Let her be your guide.

As you hold her in your arms, you will receive all you have ever needed.

There Is No Harmony Without Resonant Consonance

TOO LONG HAVE YOU QUIETED the voice of emotion within you, both the laughter and the cries. Too long have you tried to tame the spirit of who you are, of the child you left abandoned in your hurry to grow up. You wanted to take life seriously and leave behind the frivolity of youth.

Still, that child is waiting to greet you and throw her arms around you.

Some are tentative. Some are joyous. Some stand at the periphery and wait to be ushered in. Others race toward you, unbridled with enthusiasm. They look up, eager to receive your direction, and when you see them you know what to do.

You remember a place and time, in the world of physical reality or in the world of your imagination, where you felt safe and loved, as if you had always belonged. Go there now. Take the child you were with you. Show him the way.

Are you there?

Take in the sights and sounds, the miracles unfolding in every direction, coming clear right before your eyes. More than one child may appear. Welcome all. Sit together in a circle and know this: all is well.

This is the point of beginning. This is the moment outside time, the place of unlimited possibility. Begin and begin again. You are awake now, and in wholeness, you take your first breath, ushering in a new experience of what it means to truly live.

Come together and live as one.

The Wonder of Seeing through New Eyes

THROUGH THE EYES of a newborn babe, you see clearly now the limitations that have always been. Time expands outward in ever-widening circles of trust. Trust in the here and now. Trust in what has always been. Trust in what is becoming even now.

And the feeling of your magical place is rooted within the soul.

It is an ever-expanding universe where you can become. What's it like? Are there rainbows and waterfalls or a summer field? Are there butterflies and unicorns? A scene right out of the Jetsons? Whatever it is, smile. You have envisioned a world to which you will always belong.

In the beginning, you were. In the beginning, I am.

Speak! Speak a soliloquy of syllables. Sing the symphony of you. Allow it to trickle down, to bubble up, to cascade through your cells. Feel the vibration of this, "Yes!" and the resonance of the reservoir of truth welling up within.

Welcome to the world.

Eyes wide open, your hearts will now become a portal to the truth of who you've always been. Bathed fresh in these embryonic waters of life, you will emerge whole from this time of endings and take your first breaths, your first steps. You will speak your very first words in a language imprinted on your hearts before time began.

From this beautiful unfolding, peace will multiply, division be no more. And there will be no "other." Only the One. Only the dazzling sun and silver moon. Only endless sky with a billion stars.

And a twinkle in your eye.

Seeds of Recognition

We must learn to look at each other and see. Through the eyes of the soul, we must look for common seeds of divinity sprinkled in the soil of every human heart.

Our first thought must be love.

Love, like rain poured out upon the parched field of humanity, collected and channeled into hearts made barren by lifetimes of neglect. We must awaken to the realization that all is not lost.

You underestimate the capacity of love. The love within a single human heart might seem a trickle. But when it is tapped to quench the thirst of one who has forgotten the beauty of its taste, it unleashes tumbling waters.

If you could see from here the coursing rivers and the swift current of change flowing now because a single human heart chose once love, you would not hesitate to surrender all resistance to its flow.

Be the river running through the other's dry and dusty heart.

Cut right through deep canyons where a life's left echoing. Lift them up on wings of eagles. Lift them up so they can see their hearts of treasured jewels, a home for all who would fly free as one. Gaze upon them with such wonder at God's glory come to Earth.

Tend to them as little children at the moment of their birth, until they stand one day, majestic, triumphant, rising from the ash, smiling down upon the river, wearing life like colored splash of sun. Having lived lifetimes, they may feel, because you smiled upon them, that they've only just begun.

Allow What Is to Be

WE COME HERE WITH the remembrance of and the desire for perfection. So many of us are roused to anger at seeming injustice when we see another suffer needlessly or stumble over the same roadblocks, often the direct result of our collective choice in modern society. Others become consumed with a grief so global they lose their own way as they mourn what used to be.

To work for change is noble and just.

Yet, neither blaming the other nor losing self to the deep waters of suffering leads forward. As we raise awareness and point the way in love, there comes a point where we must allow what is to be. In doing so, we need not conform our lives.

Nor must we sacrifice higher ideals.

You show one way through and forward in the roads you choose to follow. Live simply and simply live, allowing space for all forms of expression and experience, trusting others to make the choice to do the same. And if they do not do so, choose to honor their choice not to choose.

Decide to let it be and to be who you choose to be.

Choosing Now

FREEDOM COMES IN CHOOSING NOW. When we surrender fear, we cast off the illusion that giving more means we will not have enough. Love remains exponential in its reach. And if you are the only one then you are the only one.

Expand to fill the space. Or be the desert rose.

You've heard the saying, "Bloom where you are planted." Do not wait for the right time, for the right environment, for the right circumstances to fall into place.

Be here now. Be now here. And, if you are nowhere, then be there and know you are loved. And know you are love. And know love. Know there is no thing greater than love. Love is there. Always, there is love.

Feel it rising up within you in this moment.

Believe it to be there in the other. Believe it with so firm a conviction that you can make no choice but love. Love one another. Love when there is no cause for love. Be the cause of love. Be the causeway.

Give life a reason to believe.
Believe there is a reason.

Where's Your Sense of Humor?

YOU TROUNCE THROUGH YOUR WHOLE LIVES serious and dutiful and miss the punch line. You start as little children and, if others are fulfilling their purpose, your sole purpose is to play, to laugh, and to tap a deep reservoir of joy.

Sadly, many of you actually mastered this first class but were then misdirected by your own parents and certainly by society. You were told to behave and play follow the leader. Problem is, the self-appointed leaders were moving in small circles. It is truly funny to watch it from afar.

But it breaks you.

See if you can go back before the dour deciders directed you on a path altogether palatable but bland and boring. Can you remember the pure joy of greeting the dawn? Can you remember when you knew, unequivocally and without a moment's hesitation, that life was a surprise every day?

Now, some of you arrived here and were so awake upon your arrival that you were quite literally terrified of what you found in this place. Jolted into the reality that this life would be no picnic, you hit the panic button and begged with your very souls to go back. But there is no going back.

When you're here, you are here. So make the best of it.

If you have been sad, give yourself a comedy hour. Every day. Seek curiosity. Do the chicken dance. Laugh out loud at this upside-down world spilled out like a box of toys in a toddler's play room. Insist on finding pleasure. Resist the urge to wallow in the plentiful pain. In short, get a sense of humor.

Look Up!

IF YOU NEED A LITTLE HELP, lie on the ground in silence and watch the clouds roll by. There's a free show every day, every hour on the hour and most any other time you take the time to see.

Every morning, the sun comes up.
Every night, the sun goes down.

Clouds dance upon the stage of your world, shape-shifting and becoming. Who says the only applause needs to come from the thundering heavens?

Up here, we're content and thoroughly entertained.
You seem oblivious to the magic of it all.

Quick, there's a show starting right now.
Want to catch it?

This is Your Message in a Bottle

THE SHORES OF YOUR WORLD are filled with reminders of how deeply you are loved. It's as if, in your lives, you are walking along a beach, literally stumbling over bottle after bottle, each capped and containing a precious message of assurance and protection. They appear one after the other, piling up layer upon layer.

And you never even bother to look down.

Few are the ones who stop and realize at all that someone somewhere is trying to get a message through. Fewer still are the number among you who bother to pop the cork and read the message. It is rare indeed to find one whose heart is ready to receive the abundant truth.

SOS: *You are loved beyond measure.*

There are endless oceans filled with wave after wave rising and falling with this resounding message. Let it wash over you. Let it change your world. I hope you're getting the message. When you do, pass it on.

And pick up the bottles, will you?

Discombobulated by Direction

YOU ARE ACCUSTOMED TO THINKING of direction in terms of up and down, left and right. You see them as opposites. Go left, and you cannot enjoy the mysteries in the field to your right. Look down too long and the story goes that you may well lose sight of heaven and be doomed to a life dimmed by darkness. You confuse yourselves.

You are only at the beginning.

Human civilization has advanced at a rapid pace. You live in a time of tremendous technological advancement. And yet you still see your own lives as limited. You believe following a particular path cuts you off from what you might experience had you taken another way.

Think of life as multidimensional reality.

An expanding sphere of infinite possibilities exists in the container of a single moment. You simply are not equipped to see it, because you have been conditioned by defining descriptors of direction.

Up in Smoke

SOMETIMES, BY THE TIME YOU CHOOSE to be here now, you find yourself out of time. And all seems to be going, going, gone. Up in smoke.

Sometimes life passes quickly and is gone before we even saw the opportunity it presented us.

Some of us arrive at a point of disillusionment. We feel the fire waning within us. We sense the flicker of time passing by. We see the sudden flash of all that has been left unsaid or undone.

Perhaps we lose hope. Perhaps we lose our way.

But all is never lost, and the way is always opening up. Where we see the last ember, life rises up unseen from ash and raises us to greater possibility than we could ever have imagined for ourselves.

Ashes to Ashes

IT'S NOT THE END OF THE STORY. It's merely chapter one. We begin. And then we begin again. And, while we have always seen death as leaving those whom we loved in this lifetime, we do not leave them at all unless we so choose.

Our essence remains.

The love with which we loved while here is carried forward. We are not found beneath some marker in the ground that records the dates of our birth and passing to the new birth so neatly. We are found in the heart of the great I Am, the eternal birth, an infinite love for all that is and is becoming. There is no too early or too late, no life extinguished. There is only changing form.

There is no was, only is. What once was is now.

You need not see the log on the fire to be warmed in this life. The physical is but one aspect of reality. Seeing is not the whole of believing.

We are here. Let your hearts beat with this truth.

We are the lights that shine when you fear your light has dimmed. When your fire burns out and all seems lost, gone up in smoke, we rise with you to celebrate your awaited birth and rejoice in perfect timing.

Grace Unfurls Its Wings

World without end, you are cradled in an infinite grace, an indestructible nest of love. And, even as you fly far from it and fall from its comfort, love expands to hold you in its wide embrace. You are winged ones, migrating even now back to your native home. Rest in the truth that you have never been far.

A heartbeat from remembering, you are where love is to be reborn again. Your life is the reincarnation of this truth.

Love has not died. No matter your perception that all has been lost. Notwithstanding the darkness that surrounds you. Never mind the long stretches of shadow that have wrapped around the girth of your world.

Rekindle now the light of love inextinguishable.

Hope is not lost where love is found, and love can be found—even in the vast expanse of space and time, seemingly emptied of all that is, yet filled with infinite grace and possibility.

Surrender to that grace and you become love.

Life is the Cradle

MANY OF YOU HAVE all you need but lack trust—trust that life is working for your good, always. Trust that you are loved, safe and protected. This condition has arisen from the instability you have experienced, usually as a little child.

Let life be your cradle now.

Look around for the evidence that life is working in your favor. Observe nature and the natural condition. See how the March lilies spring up through the crusted snow. Observe and then participate in the dance of the changing seasons.

See how life unfolds its blanket of comfort in unexpected ways.

The Infinite Now

BEING PRESENT DOES NOT LIMIT your experience. It expands it to infinite proportions. When you bring yourself fully to the present, you open up entire realms of being and knowing. You gain access to immeasurable truths that can guide you in the next instant and in the very moment in which you find yourself.

Only when you are fully here can you be there.
Or anywhere at all.

There are ways of seeing time and space: the past, the present and the future, for example. Here, there, near, far—do not define yourself merely by such measures.

Release now the illusion of limitation.

There are no lines that cannot be crossed, for the line itself was created. There is no value except the value that we place in it. The truth of who you are is not divided into increments of time. The wholeness of you is contained in every fragment, in each imperfect representation of who you are.

See yourself as uncontained, unbound by such delineations and descriptors.

All in All

You are all in all. You are all. All is well. You are well. See yourself as so, as having been and as becoming still.

You are life, and life is you.

Not just in you. Not just around you. You are not separate from all that is, and All That Is resides within you. And you bring it to its fullest expression.

We can never fully capture all of who we are, for we quickly expand beyond the confining limits of mere definition. This is because we are a creative force.

We are creators.

And so you cannot be reduced to the sum total of your experience. You are not the product of your past and present circumstance. You exist outside the equation of the future that you or others have predicted or envisioned for you.

Markers

No mistake, however grave, can be your grave unless you choose it to be so. You are not at the end unless you limit yourself by labeling yourself a failure, a mistake.

You are not that.

You exist outside the bounds of what result you have helped produce by right or wrong thinking. There may be a reason why, but do not allow that reason to define who you are, for it is only partial and not the whole.

So do not bother with the why.

Focus, rather, on the why not. Knowing why something has been is useful, but asking of the present and future why not rather than dissecting the why of the past pulls us toward the recognition that we are always becoming more of who we are.

Mark the time by moving through it.

Weather

LIFE CAN BE DEVASTATING. It can turn in a second. It can be frightening. And it is always extraordinarily beautiful if we choose to make it so.

We always have the choice.

There is nothing that can happen. No storm, unexpected turn of the screw, and no unforeseen accident or tragedy can separate us from one another as spiritual beings. Nothing can separate us from the love that is God or from God who is love.

We will always be held in that love. We will always exist.

That will never be taken from us. We may not exist in physical form in this world. We may not have the same capacity that we once had. Our lives may not look like we had thought they would or once intended them to be.

We are. Love is.

Down Came the Rain

YOU SEE YOURSELVES AS SMALL, insignificant—the tiny spider weaving its home in a quaint corner of the world. It is beautiful, and you are happy for a time. But then you see you have climbed up a water spout, and life's deluge washes you out unexpectedly.

Again, all seems lost.

Rain or shine, you experience yourself as alone, displaced. Rain or shine, you shiver at the cruelty of nature, the twists of fate that require you to begin again. You feel you are always searching for your home—for what you think you had. You can't find your way back to that water spout that was your home. And all you can remember is the endless rain that washed out the dreams you had for your life.

But you are not designed to cling to the safety of obscurity.
You are meant to weave a home of beauty.

The sun may shine its rainbow light through the droplet of water resting in the crevice of silken threads that intersect the circumference of your new abode.

And up comes the sun.

It shines down at the precise moment a child passes by, looks up and sees whole worlds reflected there. And that remembrance of the rain that swept your world away fades as new worlds are born in another because you found the faith to weave again.

And the world becomes a better place.

No Compromise

YOU MAY SEE YOUR LIFE as compromised—something less than it could have been. Or should have been or might have been.

But somewhere it is altogether possible that some beautiful soul may find the courage to fly again simply because you refused to curl up in the corner and drown in the tears you would have cried amid the devastation.

This is the pain of childbirth and the tender mercy of becoming.

It is the miracle of conception and the unfathomable grace of second chances. Love may come again to the world, and that love may come into being beyond your awareness and outside the depth of your field of perception.

But because that love is come, humanity itself is healed all the more.

New life grows where once only nubs on tired branches formed to shield the few drops of sap left deep within the core. And, after a time, the passion of life itself stirs, gathering momentum, bursting forth eventually into a glorious spring.

Beauty unto Beauty

AND ALL THESE THINGS are connected.

They began in the imperceptible seeds of faith, hope and love—in the potential, the perfection, and the wholeness caught up in the storm you could have called the end. Beautiful ones, you may never know when you choose to begin again what worlds of wonder might unfold, what beauty might be born from the simple courage you found to say, "Yes" to your life.

And, in time, when you are changed in an instant, the weight of this world will slip effortlessly from you.

You will stand amazed at the good you have done and at the life that continues to unfold because you gave thanks for the breath of being and then gathered up all the strength you had and proclaimed,

"It is enough."

Though your results seemed meager and paled in comparison to the heights of glory you had hoped to attain, you will see one day the cascading abundance that rushed out in every direction, infusing the world with the grace to carry on. Blessed are you.

You may never know how many lights shine because you are.

Trail Mix

WE DON'T SET OUT KNOWING what's in store for us in this journey we call life. We carry a bit of trail mix in our pocket—something to snack upon.

And sometimes that is more than enough. Then, almost without warning, we find ourselves standing on a new frontier, on the line between all we have ever known and the field of our future. We see rivers making their way to a sea of untapped potential, of dreams we never knew we had.

In these moments, we may reach into our pockets for our meager bag of trail mix and convince ourselves we are totally unprepared and incapable of making such an arduous journey into the great unknown. And then some of us dare to take a single step in a new direction and find…

A mystery. A miracle.

The full measure of magnificence contained within a moment. Life rises up to meet us on our way, and we are surprised. Pack your trail mix, but fix your eyes on the way that opens up when you dare to step out of your comfort zone and into a new story.

Belonging

BELOVED, YOU BELONG TO ALL THAT IS. You are that I am. I am that you are. You long for a deeper connection and a life of purpose, a place to belong.

Be longing, then. In the longing for, you belong to.

As you reach for something more, know this: you have all you have ever needed. You belong to an infinite supply.

So, let it rain and let it go. Let it be.

Always know you are held within our love,
as we are held within your hearts.

Trajectory

MANY OF YOU ENCOUNTER A MOMENT that is magical and meet the image of all that is possible for you magnified in the mirror of another. Usually, this occurs when you happen upon one you did not expect to find here, in this place, in this time.

And then, just as quickly as you found it, the magic is over and the glaring lights come on just before you take the stage, blinding you. Or maybe the leading man or lady walks off stage, leaving you looking like a fool, standing in the spotlight with nothing to stay.

You grieve as unseen forces tear at your hearts and pull you apart.
Worlds are lost.

Still, you do not forget. You have been changed forever by the soul of another, in which you have seen yourself whole, at peace, loved beyond measure. It seems to you senseless that such a thing could be seized, held hostage or taken back by the universe almost before you could catch your breath.

Your hearts, after what seemed a single beat of wholeness,
break with their every beat.

And, despite the purest desire to return to that place where you belong, life's trajectory, set by the free will of all involved, will not allow it.

Shooting Stars

EVEN THOUGH YOU SEE there may be no hope of restoration to your rightful home with the other, you circle round the dark side of the moon. You hold fast to that flicker of light, that singular moment when you saw your selves as once you were.

Though one remembers and one does not, there will come a time when you shall meet again, your hearts collide to spark a memory lost to the one.

Carry on!

Truth can survive the longest lie. In time, day is always born of night. Love remains untainted by another's willful dismissal of its shocking interruption of some presumed master plan.

Ripped from the very love you've searched all your life to find, you fly blind on through the night afraid you will lose your mind. But it doesn't matter. Let the rise and fall of your chest be enough.

Let love be the fuel that hurtles you through the loneliest years.

Let it go. Let all your love rush out before you to meet the void, and know this: love is never lost.

Make your way, believing what gift has been bestowed will be returned tenfold, and what seems forever ending will find at last its new beginning.

Have faith in beauty, and believe that it may rise again.

The Home Stretch

TRAVEL LIGHT. GOOD BOOTS, good friends, and the gift of solitude on an easy Sunday morning are all you really need.

Breathe in that sweet whisper of a dream, and breathe out all that would keep you from believing in it. Just breathe. And if you fall down, get back up again.

You are on your way, and you have come further than you think.

There's a long stretch where the dust is kicked up and you're not even sure you are on your way home. In fact, you have almost arrived.

You may think it's over. You may say there's no chance you won't be thrown out at the plate and lose the game for your team. Wait and see.

Do you believe in miracles?

Double Dares and Life on the Leading Edge

HOW DARE YOU? How dare you wound one who has yet to find her wings? How dare you take your reckless single shot and silence a song the world will never know?

And, you, sweet spirit, how dare you fall from the sky without a fight for who you are? How dare you lie there on the ground and forget you knew to fly?

How dare you collude with one another and conspire to snuff out the very light that led you to where you are? How dare you?

Life dares to believe in you. Dare to believe in it.

I dare you.

Forever and This Day

ON THE ONE HAND, IT IS TRUE that you have all the time you need, forever and a day. There is no end in the way you have perceived it. There is no hurry. There is only the one decision before you.

What will you choose this day?

What word will you speak?
What reality will you create with the thoughts you think?

Will you choose to open the gift of the moment that comes to greet you? Will you remain oblivious to it? Or will you shove it to the back of the closet, hedging your bets that if you do this tomorrow will show up with something better.

Love what is.

Live in the fullest possible way, into the gift of this moment.

Like clockwork the days come one after the next, and you become accustomed to the ticking of time. And you never even know how sweet it is.

Don't be in such a hurry to get through this day and on to the next.

Take your time.
Celebrate.

Telling Truth in a Tone-Deaf World

YOUR DAYS ARE FILLED with much that is unnecessary. You make much ado about nothing. You are bombarded with noise that clouds and confuses. You subject yourself and succumb to the onslaught.

There are those who speak truth among you, but you have grown hard of hearing. You tire of changing stations, of tuning in and tuning out to the turn of the trick. You grow weary of attending the exposition of the fraudulent and the famous of the moment.

You search endlessly for truth and yet you fear both knowing it and not knowing it.

You see yourselves as jaded, jilted one too many times, left standing at the altar of confession. And so you stammer into silence, numbing yourselves with too much spice of life.

Or you stimulate yourselves with sounds of static, silence, or smashing symbols, depending on the day—anything you presume might substitute for the voice of truth you alternatively seek and avoid. You tell yourselves truth has vanished from your world.

Listen. Really listen, and then tell me what is true.

The Speed of Light

A BILLION SOULS have come and gone. Who are you to say that not a single one of them burns in midnight sky for you?

Should you cross your arms, close your eyes and choose to walk alone, your diamond of a star that lights your way is, of course, lost to you. And the song you are meant to sing is swallowed up before you've learned its tune.

You are safe. Uncross your arms.

Open your heart to all you are deserving of, just because you are. Practice this a little at a time until the day you can hold your palms open to the Earth, releasing any pain you have experienced and then turn them toward the sky to receive all the love you'll ever need. Reach them out and touch the life of another who may or may not see you there.

Love travels at the speed of light.

Forgiving

LIFE IS FOR GIVING, nothing more. Nothing less than letting go will do. In this world and the next, there are those who would give their lives that you would be free. Among you, there are also those who would bind you to their truth—a truth they believe has already set them free.

Some know the harm they do, and do it anyway.

Others have fooled themselves into believing they do what they do to you for your highest good. They have made themselves to be gods on Earth, blindfolding themselves willingly to all that is unfinished in their own hearts.

No matter your age, no matter your heritage, no matter your position in spirit or society, your soul cannot be bound without your full consent.

Say you will guard your hearts and minds.

Let no man make a prison of your body or take prisoner your soul. Refuse to be held captive by another, no matter how much you love them or how wise you think them to be.

Likewise, turn.
Escape from all that would make you into a jailer of your own soul.

Nourish body, mind and spirit. Neither starve nor stuff them. Neither repress any one of them nor give the one free rein above the others. Make peace with who you are.

Bind up your broken heart.
Know yourself as the free spirit that you were created to be.

Origin and Originality

WE COME FROM GOD, who is our home.

On Earth, we are born to parents and imprinted with patterns of life. We carry bits and pieces and are, in fact, immersed in the streams of soul shared with all of humanity.

Though we originate in the mind of God and in the womb of our mother, we come bearing fine gifts of original design. You are no designer knock-off.

Give up your search for some label, some stamp of approval.

Set your own value. Declare your worth, and live as if you mean it. Make it clear *you* matter to you, for you are no victim of circumstance.

Willingly you gave yourself and gave of yourself, once upon a time, to take shape and form. And now you are the maker of your life, the champion of your cause. Life is your canvas.

What will fill your blank page, your stage, your silver screen?

The Dream We Dreamed

THERE ONCE WAS A DRY LAND, parched desert, with the dusty particles of a dream that had died blowing about in the void. There once were a people wandering—nomads, thirsty and longing for a life they could no more recall. Burned beneath a blazing sun by day, shivering beneath the cold of night, they survived day to night to day.

Always walking, stumbling, tripped by the sands of time.

Delirious and waking to a common dream of an ocean oasis, they continued on a never-ending quest for something they had forgotten. Until the day they died to lack and drank their fill from an abundance of stars smiling down upon them.

And, in an instant, out of nothing, flowed a river. It sprang forth from nothing but a single choice to believe in goodness. The ground gave way to the expression of what they imagined. And then:

A miracle. One river became two, and two became four.
And four became sixteen. And the land became as fertile as their hearts.

This was the dream we dreamed and the way, once, we walked upon the land. And now the whole Earth is curled up, like a tiny infant inside each one of us. Eyes closed but becoming more and more aware, both of her grounding in a Universe far greater than herself and also of her own life and skin, she begins to flex her muscles. Her heart beats with the desire to soar.

Mother Earth is waking. We must hold her now.

We must soothe her with our song. When she wails, care for her. When she cannot seem to rest, sit by her side. Thank her for the gift she brings. Share with her the treasures of your heart, the ideas that come to your mind.

Remember the dream we dreamed, and give back to her,
with gratitude for all she has given to you.

Reaching for Rivers of Hope

REMEMBER THE LITTLE KID running through the city, following the red balloon? Be like this child. As you keep focused on the goal of waking up, you will attract greater visibility. People will see what you are chasing after. And as more and more of you focus on that red balloon, momentum will shift.

Feel the joy of jumping up for that elusive promise.
It will lead you to all you need to find.

There are layers within layers of awakening, rivers that lead deeper and deeper. These multiplied rivers will spring forth from your hearts. Your heart is the source of the source from which love and life flow. As more and more of you open your hearts, miracles will spill out, creating an ever-increasing flow of abundance. The rivers are an unfolding promise of pathways to joy, bubbling brooks to remind you of what you have always held within your hearts.

You see, the desert you have wandered in is the true mirage. And, too, as a people you have become accustomed to shielding your eyes and stumbling forward, chasing after all that has seemed so illusive.

And there it is!

Stop. Stop the endless search.
Just breathe.

Then, breathe more deeply. Be still and know. You know what you know when you need to know it, and this is the time to know. There is no more quest, and your questions need no answers.

Ssshhh. Hear all that will come to you in the silence.

In the sweet surrender to the here and now, you will embrace the mystery of all time. In the slow breathing in, you will find the fragrant flowering of your dream. And as you close your eyes, you will see for the first time the wonder of this world and be filled with the need for nothing more.

In the experience of this moment flowing into the next, your faith that this is indeed possible will spring a river of hope from which will flow a tumbling waterfall of love, bringing healing and new growth where you thought all had died.

And from these buds of promise, passion is reborn.
And, through it all, you will know beauty.

You will recognize yourselves anew and see yourselves grow into the full beauty of who you have always been.

Ebb and Flow

IN EVERY FALL, THERE IS A RISING—the seeds of momentum that lie within, the gathering up of all that has survived the brutal winds of change. And then there is a moment of the turning—that swift influx of pure, essential life force.

When we surrender to that life force, once again we throw our arms wide open and lean into possibility. We allow the wind to carry us until again the time seems right and we find our legs beneath us and set a course for ourselves in the direction of another spring.

There is an ebb and flow.

You become like a chorus of frogs singing in the swamp of the unknown. They croak out of the simple conviction that they are and that conviction rises through the fog of confusion. Each voice is distinct and yet expanding in an echo of unity that rises through the long night.

Raise your voice to find your truth.

Soon the truth itself will reverberate within you and lead you forward. The croaking will become the song of beginning again. Your voices will sound out together.

Together, you will awaken the new world.

Staying Current

IMAGINE A RIVER. Floating, you have passed the sudden bend. Ahead you see yet another twist in the winding river's course. You are not looking back, not anticipating. Just staying with the current, allowing yourself to be carried forward naturally, laughing with the joy of the river's flow.

You may have been told, "Don't make waves."

But you do make waves. You are meant to make waves, because you are, in fact, a wave. You are dancing light, moving through space and time, expanding, changing shape, taking form—always becoming.

Stop holding back. Stop pulling against the tide.

Stop clinging to the shore. Stop resisting letting go. Say yes to the unknown that is far on a distant horizon and rush into it.

Life is here.

Life is having kissed the shore and allowed yourself to let go and to be pulled back into a vast ocean of experience.

Distillation

Clouded by chemistry of obligation, the elemental essence of love has gone into hiding. Distillation is in order.

But you must consent to allow your heart to undergo this change.

You must find within you, individually and collectively, a willingness to endure the flame, allowing the release of toxins and impurities that have too long polluted the waters of your world.

Allow this purifying fire. Surrender.

Know your essential self undivided, purest properties protected, will remain. Quintessential selves restored, you will return again to your natural state of being and cultivate from the core the seeds of soul that hold the promise of potentiality.

Maybe You're Just Rusty

WORN OUT, BEATEN DOWN, you can see you're in a field of dreams.

But you don't know how to move.
You don't know which direction to take.

You think you've lost your heart, because you've lost your way.

You've become the tin man, stiffened by circumstance, feeling, perhaps, hollowed out by having lost your chance to cast off all your cares and dance your way to where your heart has always longed to be.

But maybe you're just rusty.
And maybe you have all you need.

Breath

THE THING IS, YOU CAN CHOOSE to change your life in every breath in and in every breath out. Breathe in spirit. If you don't inspire you may well expire in one form or another.

So just breathe.

Breathe in the assurance that you are not alone but are instead intimately and infinitely connected to all that is. Breathe out all that would keep you apart from the truth of your essence.

Deep, focused breathing will take you back to truth.
Practice it. Follow it.

When the sun rises, give thanks with your breathing and welcome the day. When the sun sets, allow your breathing to return to grateful appreciation. Give thanks with the rise and fall of your chest and know that you have all you have ever needed and all you ever will.

Allow your body to open fully to your breath, expanding to welcome the flow of life.

Feel it fill up each chamber and then move deeper within you. Expand as a balloon, filling the throat and chest, then allowing your breath to fill your mid-section and move down and down into the base of your spine and the root of your being.

Feel the wonder of life with every breath.
Take not one for granted.

Born Free

WE ENSLAVE ONE ANOTHER and ourselves when we create false hierarchies and prop ourselves up as gods and rulers of kingdoms of our own creation.

There is but one kingdom—the kingdom of God.

There is but one creation, connected as a whole and magically sprinkled throughout the Universe in a million special varieties.

We are born equally free, created from the same stuff,
no one any more special than the other.

If we are born free, then we are meant to live free and to uphold the value of freedom. The Creator calls us to honor and protect the sacred freedom in which and for which we are created.

How are you doing with that?

Retrieval

IF YOU HAVE LOST YOUR WAY or lost sight of the full flame of freedom, all is not lost. The way back is to see the holy in the ordinary. In fragments of time and in the people passing by, look for the miracle.

Believe and seek to see again.

Your sight will be restored as you recommit to acts of soul retrieval that begin with simple observation.

Two minutes a day can lead you into ten and then you will find an hour has passed and your heart has been held in harmony with the hallowed Earth and heaven has come closer than you ever knew it to be. And the free hours will be magnified into days and then sweeping vistas of freedom unfolding to infinity.

Retrieval begins with a single choice to reach within and reconnect with a core essence you may not at first remember.

Trust that it is there. Listen to the stillness.

Be with you without the trappings of the life you think to be free. Release them all and come fully present to all that is unknown.

Know you are, and soon you will begin to understand who you are.

Flix

WHAT IF IT WERE JUST A MOVIE? What if everything you saw mirrored in reality was playing out on a big screen?

Because it is. For your entertainment.

Did you forget that only you decide whether to redeem your ticket for the show? Maybe it's time for some new movies.

Let's go old school and start with the talkies. Or, better yet, let's go back to before the soundtrack put our minds to sleep.

The essential artistry of silent movies was in capturing the range of human motion and emotion, frame by frame by frame. Now, your movies are a blur, as if you couldn't get enough in real life.

Let's rewind. Let's go reel to real.

Back in the screening room, much as we up here might like to edit the "reality," you are the producers of your lives. You direct the actors on your stage.

You choose your own soliloquy. You choose what play is to be or not to be. You call, "Action!" and set things in motion.

You choose when to call the scene or do another take.

Flex

FLEXIBILITY BEGINS WITH FLEX. Before you can exercise your ability to choose the reality you create in your hearts or in your world, you must choose to use the muscle of your mind.

Let's boil it down:
Mind over matter.

I don't know if you've thought of this before, but if you want to be a body in motion, you might want to master the art of the move. Now, calm down. You don't even have to do an entire revolution.

Flow in your life begins with the flex.

Try it. Flex the muscle of your mind. Let your actions follow in its footsteps. If you don't like where you are or where you find yourself to be, get a different routine.

Change your mind.

Flux

THE INFLUX OF MIND MASTERY, coupled with a return to your heart's essence—*to love*—will carry you back into the current. And therein lies the present. It is a cycle of giving and receiving that knows no end. This leads us to the inception of change in you as the exception to the rule.

The rules say you should, you must and stay within these lines.

The rules only became necessary when you forfeited your inner knowing and refused to give way to the turn of the season, to the necessity of change. And then your rules created a false dichotomy between those of you who fell in line, who took your marching orders and fit into society and those of you who rebelled against the rigidity of what felt false but then also found yourselves outside the mainstream.

Many who followed dutifully wake to find themselves far from dreams they thought had died.

Too few of you who resisted have persisted. Some who have persisted in following the beat of their own drums have by now wandered so far afield that their voices have been lost or muffled to mere murmur.

Thus, the heartache of humanity.

The Moving Spiral Staircase

LIFE IS ALWAYS MOVING US, shifting to the left or right, elevating us or taking us down a few notches. We have to adjust. There are incremental movements we must make as we approach our goal. Sometimes, that means stepping up. Other times, it's just a small adjustment—a pivot left or right.

Viewed from far away, we can see the beautiful slope of our ascension.

You come so close to the next world and barely recognize that you have moved at all. You have been lifted into the realms of angels, but because you find yourself sitting in the same chair or lying beneath your comforter you distrust this.

You convince yourself it was just a dream.
Or not possible, because here you are.

There are two complementary paths we travel as we pass through this life. There is the outer life, the world of weathering the world—its elements, the relationships we form, the work we choose to do, the external challenges and joys. And there is the inner life where, if we are lucky, we begin to see sprouts of growth, new awareness, expanded trust in ourselves, and an ever-widening love for our own humanity.

As you love what is, you move toward the unfolding awareness
of all that has been.

Curve Speed

SOMETIMES YOU SEE the long slope of the curve ahead. We know we are transitioning into a stretch of life's highway that leads us gently into something new.

We see a little of the way ahead and it looks inviting.

The curve seems manageable, something we have waited for; we think we've got it handled. You believe you are ready—that this is nothing. And so you hit the gas, in a hurry to get around the bend and see what's on the other side.

Take care of the curves. Give yourself the time to ease into them.

There is something to be said for slow and steady. Take the turn too fast and you wipe out, losing more than just a little time.

A Cup of Coffee

You have been conditioned to change lanes quickly, to pursue forward progress—onward and upward to the golden gates of some desired final destination.

Presumably, upon arriving, you will know you are there.

But in your haste to get where you are going, don't miss the scenery.

Sit down and have a cup of coffee. You never know who you might meet, who might see you smile and let that be enough to carry them through another day.

One fine day you might just discover someone smiling back at you. And that might just change the course of your life and put you on the road again to where you were always meant to be.

So, get some coffee. Stay awake for the journey.

Love life's ride.

Traffic

When something blocks your flow as you move through your life, there are really two choices.

The first is to grit your teeth and push through at a grinding pace. This will wear you down and wear you out.

It will make you old before your time.

The other choice is to pull off the road, take a detour or find a way around, not through.

This may delay the gratification of your arrival at the time you deem best. But you will nonetheless arrive and show up in an undeniably better mood than had you stayed, stuck in traffic.

Reclamation

IN YOUR WORLD, SO MUCH that was pure and nourishing has been corrupted to the degree that it is no longer safe for you. You must learn to separate out those contaminants, some invisible which naturally cling to clean energy.

The process of removing what is waste requires discernment.

Discernment requires rigorous examination of all that does not serve the truth.

To reclaim that which was bestowed upon you as a gift of grace, you must begin with gratitude. Give thanks for it. See the perfection within it. Refuse to cast it off as lost, to surrender the gift because it has been contaminated.

Instead, choose love and honor.

Then, allow that love and honor to lead you to new ideas that restore the gift to its natural state. Think, speak and share thoughts of loving-kindness toward gift and giver.

There is never a need to engage in the cycle of destruction.

Transform your thoughts. Turn your anger toward those who have been reckless with the gift into equal action for good. Breathe compassion into the sadness you feel and into your own hearts.

Envision the essence and allow what is waste to fall away.

Become an advocate for the gift and also for those who have not yet awakened to it and do all you can to support the gift and restore it to its natural state of being.

Breaking Bread

But here, you say, you have to eat. There are always hungry mouths to feed, and it is a nuisance. You tire of the mundane and the profane. And so you go through the day muttering complaint after complaint against the day and all that fills it.

You wholly miss the holy, and that there is extravagance hidden there within your ordinary.

Extraordinary. And altogether unnecessary.

When you break the bread, remember it is a gift. Your money may have purchased this particular loaf, but you have not invented bread or manifested it from thin air. Perhaps such a miracle might occur but not so long as you pat yourself on the back and recite to yourself that you have worked hard and this is all that you have.

And tomorrow you will get up and repeat the cycle.

Break the chain of pride locked so tight around your hearts and minds that you have cut yourself off from the remembrance of the bread of life broken for all of you, the manna that nourishes your body and spirit, and the grace of those gathered round your table.

Drink the new wine and get yourselves some new wineskins.

There's no cause for drivel and repetition in the presence of mystery made manifest. Get it together. Receive a bounty of blessing and give thanks for the fancy of the feast and the grace of the meager meal.

Get in the Story

ARE YOU COMFORTABLE just watching all of life unfold from a good vantage point? Have you scurried up a tree?

Do you like to live above the fray?

Look out! The big story will rush to fill the smallest hearts.
You are never beyond the reach of love. Never.

What goes up must come down.

Those who believe they've got one up on life are never as happy as they appear. Neither are they as alone as they may feel.

It does not matter who has given up on you. It does not matter that you have given up on yourself. It only matters that you come down from your perch and get in the story.

Because you are the story.

Fault Lines

ARE YOU EXPERIENCING DIVISIONS in your relationships at home or at work? Are there deep gaps in your fulfillment? Are you always sinking lower into the valley of sadness? Are your voices, like doves crying out, clashing against the canyon walls?

Is there friction? Go back in time and you're likely to find fault lines.

The moment you blamed the other a tiny crack in the foundation was formed. Over time, the blame and the shame, the contempt and endless criticism eroded the very foundation of your relationship, wearing down the solid rock.

And you became two plates, made of the same stuff
but pulled in opposite directions.

The stress became too much and what you thought would surely stand the test of time crumbled before your eyes.

Stop looking for someone else to make up for what you lack. Take responsibility for every word and every action. Surrender your desperate search to fill the holes in your life and all you think is missing from you.

Try something new. Start finding favor.

Start filling in the cracks in the foundation with love.
Plant flowers of faith, living into another spring.

Cooperation

SOME OF YOU HAVE COME TO the altogether scientific conclusion that God is not active in your world. You don't see it because you have chosen not to believe it. You formed a hypothesis and set out to prove yourself correct.

And, surprise, you did!

When you look at all the evidence gathered by all of those looking at the question, the fact of the matter appears in the form of energy, elusive but no less powerful a conclusion.

Work together, and you will see.

Surprise!

A MOMENT WILL COME that will appear, for better or worse, to have been destined. It will seem as if, for all your life, you had been on a collision course with this single moment when you come face to face with the truth. Perhaps this truth is a something.

Perhaps it is someone—your beloved or your betrayer.

This moment of truth revealed is inevitable,
but the element of surprise is not lost.

Ultimately, it's all up to you.

Will you recognize the truth or scramble to reorder entire worlds if only
to protect the sanctity of the illusion you had created for yourself?

Open the Present, Already

IT'S BEEN SITTING RIGHT THERE, forever, *hidden in plain sight*.

Will you choose to receive the full realization of what you have always known? Will you reject it outright? Or will you sit there admiring the bow and the wrapping as if that is the whole of the gift?

Some of you question why the gift should be there, thinking it must be some kind of mistake. Some have been known to grab the present, tear into it with a ferocious spirit and then just as quickly cast it aside.

The surprising truth is this:

When that moment of now arrives you are either ready or you are not. Surprisingly, it's all up to you. Do you cycle through the lessons, one by one, and move on swiftly to the next? Or do you lock horns with the devil in the detail and do battle to the death? Have you considered what is sacrificed when you insist on being right, deconstructing the truth revealed piece by piece?

You see the result before you: tattered pieces.

You forget this is merely a reflection of what you have done to your own heart and soul.

How invested are you in your choice?

How long do you want to take to learn to dance with life? There's no real hurry. Take your time to decide what kind of life you want.

Or get up from your seat and dance with destiny.

Compensation

EVERYBODY WANTS HIS DUE—some reward for having survived the fray and having made it through another day. We learn this well as little children who have arrived in a world, or a family that is our world, where we are under-appreciated or not even seen for who we truly are.

We shrink.

We set our true value aside in order to survive the harrowing passages of growing up. Knowing this to be a raw deal, we learn to compensate.

So, if we came here laughing and filled with light but found ourselves trapped in an environment where free expression was simply not permitted, we may have felt squelched, silenced, shut down or swallowed up by the serious. Maybe you were bewildered for having come to such a place as this. In such a case, one might become skilled at the art of snarkiness and sarcasm.

We become the cynic.

Or we put on the straight face like a straight jacket and perfect our act to such a degree that we take the show on the road. This is, after all, our just reward. This is the lie we tell ourselves.

Such compensation is nothing of the sort.

It robs us blind. And yet, if we are lucky, this leads us back to the stage. There, at first, we simply play out the same drama, night after night. But this very stage can become the place where we rediscover our joy and wonder.

One day, perhaps, we laugh again.

Let Me Hear Your Body Talk

WE ARE LIVING IN A MATERIAL WORLD where matter matters.

Your body gets a vote, so why do you push it away and subjugate it and say it doesn't matter? It matters. It is matter.

You are neither separate from your body nor defined by it.

You are not your body, but you are not meant to simply dwell in your body. You are meant to dance with it as a partner, to marvel at the way it moves you in this world.

*Listen to your body.
What does it want to tell you?*

What ideas does it long to express? How does it want to get you where you want to go? What can you learn from it? How might you honor it, nourish it and appreciate the very gift of it?

Out of the Hive and into the Cuckoo's Nest

BUSY BEES ARE ALL ABUZZ about the one that got away.

And should that one revolutionary bee miss the sweet honey and come back to the clan, he's sure to be stung.

The worker bee who dares to abandon his assigned post or fails to serve his queen gets labeled crazy. The world fills up with the noise of clucking that follows him, saying louder and louder that he belongs in the cuckoo's nest.

But only you know where you belong.

If you are a bee, be a bee. But not all bees are meant to drone on endlessly. There is the life sweeter than honey. Sometimes to get it, you have to leave the hive.

Aphids and Aphrodite

ZEUS THOUGHT THE OTHER GODS would be threatened by the beauty of Aphrodite. He surmised that they would be undone by jealousy. And so she was shuttled off into a loveless marriage. Punished for who she was, Aphrodite felt such pain that she turned to others and wound up hurting all the more.

Those who shove others into shadow are no more than hungry aphids that destroy the cultivated beauty of plants.

And when your beautiful spirit begins to wither, love yourself.

Go within. Love yourself first; then, make wise choices aligned with loving and valuing you.

Aphrodite, when her gifts were thought to shine too bright, began to believe the lie. She created the only way she knew to keep some part of her soul alive. She compensated for the belief she was too beautiful and would provoke jealousy. She fulfilled it.

No matter what aphids eat you alive, your essence cannot be taken.

Know that those parts of you that show up to fill the void arise to be your champions and protectors.

Thank them for coming. Love them.
Love the you they came to love.

Forgive yourself for any mis-takes that arose because who you were was not seen and valued by others—or by you yourself.

Matriculation

HERE'S THE DEAL—when you sign up for school, you're gonna go to class. Learning will happen. It's unlikely that you will ace every life test and soar through unscathed. But when you dare to show up day after day after day and do the work, it's really not about the grades.

The bells and attendance and homework grades are simply the trappings of school. The real deal is caught up in the conversation in the classroom, and that includes the conversation you are having with you, about you, in addition to the discussion of facts and figures pertinent to your reality.

Do you go through life comparing yourself to others?

Do you make a conscious or subconscious choice to subjugate who you are and conform? Do you settle for just getting by?

Do you do your work at the last possible moment?

Do you measure yourself merely by a letter on a report card or do you dare to get involved in the real work happening all around you?

It's about making it through to the day you toss the cap up in the air without succumbing to the expectation of perfection and without dropping out.

It's about learning to work in groups with difficult people. It's about stretching the bounds of what you know. It's about coming back to balance, so that you can say yes with authority to the next opportunity. It's about having compassion for yourself.

It's about finding the courage to do your best and be yourself.

Cycles of Work and Play

WORK. PLAY. SLEEP. Rinse and repeat.

It's really not that complicated.

Work is contribution. When you share your gifts and talents, you value the world and those who share it with you. You give back. Work is our gift to the world. Play is our gift to ourselves and to one another.

Rest is required for both.

Sometimes, it's important to play at work and work at play. Both are enhanced when you mix in a little rest.

Remember nap time?
Siesta makes possible the fiesta of life and work.

So, take a break.

Seeking Something

CHANGE WHAT YOU'RE LOOKING FOR and see what you find.

If nobody's ever there for you, be there for somebody and watch what happens. If there's never enough, look for all the places where there is more than enough.

If you can't seem to get a break, stop looking for one and walk in the way until you see an opening.

Seek and you will find.

So often, you stand alone on a far-off horizon and judge the world for being unsatisfactory. You're looking for something more, but you have separated yourself from the life you seek.

Stand in the stream and feel the flow.

Only then can you gain the perspective required to carry you through. Only the experience of being immersed in life gives you the qualification to assess its give and take.

The Context of Community

IT IS ONLY WHEN WE GATHER TOGETHER, we begin to see what's possible. We first understand what we do want and what we don't want in light of the contrasting experiences we discover as we connect and converse with others passing through this life.

In relationship to one another, we seek and, inevitably, we find ourselves again—whether through joy or disappointment, through faithfulness or abandonment, through bliss or brokenness.

We remember, if only in bits and pieces, that we are not here by accident.

We are our teachers, and the lesson is this: we have come for this very purpose. We have come to reawaken fully to the truth that we are the creators, the sovereign rulers and intrepid explorers of our own lives and of this world we spin with for a time.

In family and friendship we find flickers of the truth.

Whether we are loved deeply and held closely or cast out to fend for ourselves, in the substrate of every cell we know whether such an experience is resonant with the one truth or a distortion of it. We feel such things every day but only discover truth fully when we give up the damned determination to make our own way, as if we were the only ones who ever had a once upon a time.

So come together. Observe. Know what you know. Allow it to be.

Give others the grace to see what is for themselves. Deep truths cannot be hawked like silver watches from where the sidewalks meet.

Carry your truth in grace. Hold the space for them even as you direct your own life in the way the river flows.

The Music of Solitude

IN THE STILLNESS, A MELODY RISES from within.

When you walk alone, whether by choice or by losses too vast to measure, you find a way to both find and follow the music.

Alone, there can be no mistaking the sound of truth for a lost strand of conversation or background noise. One can only believe she is crazy for so long.

Listen to your soul when life leaves you on your own.

There are the keys waiting to be played.
There you will find your song.

*Once, before life sprang up around a fertile crescent lush and green,
a river ran through it.*

Here we stand at the moment of discovery.

First, we must see the river and become it. One with its essence, we will find our flow and birth worlds of wonder.

If we choose.

EMBRACING A NEW VISION

Cultivating Essence

INSIDE: Essential Questions for SEEDS Journaling Practice

DAWN RICHERSON

Stop Waiting for the Answer

STOP SEARCHING FOR THE ANSWER. Stop looking for the way. Start moving to the music of the questions.

Start walking. Allow your soul to dance.

Open your eyes to skies dappled with possibility and infuse each day with a celebration of choice.

Raise yourself. Elevate your life. Grow your soul.

Stop waiting to be lifted by the hand of heaven. Reframe the very concept of change by seeing it as not only constant but also as the predictable opportunity for some new beginning there inside of every perceived ending.

Ask the question. Know one another. Allow yourself to be vulnerable.

Dare to live the questions now.

Unlimited Direction

To this point in human history, our ideas of change have been defined by all that we have encountered along our journey through this life and the vision we see in our mind's eye.

We focus on the future and reach toward it. This is a good start we have made, but it is only a partial revelation.

This is but one fractal of time—a singular direction limited by where we have come from and where we find ourselves right now.

In truth, there is no need for reaching, for revelation is the very substrate from which patterns of change emerge. Likewise, change itself morphs and becomes multidimensional, no more limited by the shape and form of who we have been to ourselves and to others.

See yourselves as a cycle of change, works of art splashed with the life of color and the dance of the brush across canvas. You are the masterpiece and the master, the medium and the moment in which a creation is being born.

You are all, and all is you.

Direction becomes irrelevant. Commit to the dance, to everything and to no thing at all.

You have no need for remembering the words or mastering the tune, for you are the song itself and the melody rising in the wind, ever being formed and finding your resting place in the place the song was born.

Search and Rescue

SO, ASK NOT. *Know what you know.*

Allow yourselves to be revealed and revel in the knowing and the being known, the sacredness of both the dawn of understanding and the shadow lands. Redefine value. Value redefinition.

Find a way forward, yes. But also your way back.

And into the layers of soul that blossom into possibility for ways you have not yet imagined. Trust the ripples of love to become waves that cannot drain you of you anymore than the ocean can lose its life by kissing golden shores. Knowing you've no need for replenishment, see also that nothing is lost or wasted. No one is lost to herself. You are not in need of saving.

You long for restoration, for salvation, for all to be set aright.

In the mirror, you see a stranger to your self, a life turned topsy-turvy, trunks of treasure sunken.

This is mere illusion, the inverse of hope, a mirage of shipwrecked dreams. Flip the image and you have a voyage of extraordinary wealth and cause for celebration at the discovery that life is a dance within a dream we chose.

Call off your search for one another.

See at last the beauty of your being where you are. Or where you have perceived yourself to be. Fall into being born to the miracle of a kaleidoscope of change. Soar beyond your sights of heaven and ground yourselves in the very being of who you are, indivisible and also making way for generations of possibility waiting for emergence —here when you abandon the short-sightedness of emergency.

Time Passages

THERE IS THE TIME YOU HAVE KNOWN by the ticking of a clock, and there is another experience of time that is much different. You speak of time standing still. This is sacred time, a moment infused with the promise and fulfillment of a lifetime.

The truth is you have all the time you need.

Not only is there no need for hurry; there is also no need to wait. The time is always now, and there is always time. And that time appears to meet your need. It also slips by if you choose not to live fully into it.

Redeem your ticket to ride, and take all the time you need.

Parallels in Space and Time

IMAGINE THE ANCIENT PYRAMID, a golden home for souls transitioning, safe passage made more comfortable by reminders of a ruler's riches and reward.

See now you, here and now, awakening to the all that is.

You are a cup filled from center point of stillness that provides an abundant opening to the inner life facilitated by whispers of our remembered home beyond.

A tear in the fabric of your star-crossed universe or a gaping wound inside the human heart: they are one and the same.

Mirror images are two halves of a whole, yet whole within the halves. This pattern replicates. Light is never diminished within the particles transformed as they transform the worlds they inhabit.

Into infinite darkness, light speeds its love.

Love rushes in to spark a flame, revealing colors of life reflected in the glow of all that is. Embrace it. Release it.

Breathe the promise revealed in the rise and fall of your body, caressed by every breath.

Unveiled

ON EARTH SO MANY OF YOU who have had a glimpse of the hereafter choose to see it as separate from and other than. And then there are those of you who are more awakened, and yet, you, too, would cast aside the world that is your home in favor of the home you left behind.

But this world is a world waiting to be born, held within the very womb of heaven's grace. And you must be born to it first and allow its divine splendor to be revealed in due time.

You come to Earth and are immersed in the slower yearning to become.

Some of you grow impatient, for the veil between the truth within your hearts and its very beating is thin. You are blessed, and yet you remain blinded to the beauty of being where you are. Others live in the here and now as if walking through a fog of forget-fulness. You have forgotten what you know: that on this journey, you yourself are the gift and the giver.

You yourself gave up everything you knew to receive it all again. And here you resist receiving the very gift you asked for. Wake up!

When you catch a single ray of truth, allow it to pierce that veil of separateness you have pulled between you here and you there. It is merely something you have used to fool yourself, to shield your soul from a truth you think might kill you. In fact, it will bring you back to the full and abundant life waiting for you where you are.

We are never really alone.

We are connected in a matrix of soul, uniquely formed with intricate diversity and woven into whole worlds of universal love. It is the kaleidoscope of life, patterns being rearranged to the delight of the one gazing through the looking glass and diving in to where we have always belonged.

Interior Design

DECORATE YOUR INNER LIFE with crisp thinking and feeling. Just as you would make your bed with the best quality sheets you can afford, spare no expense and handpick only the best thoughts—those that make you feel luxurious, loved for the legacy you are.

Brighten up your inner space. Shed a little light.

Clean out the dusty corners. And, while you're at it, set the mood. Get a little ambience. Spruce up your soul, because whether you know it or not, you've got company. Guess who's coming for dinner? And lunch and breakfast, too? You are!

So fill your heart with delicious experience.

Include a few good books and ideas. Invite the prophets of old and modern-day pioneers to join you. Set your table in the wilderness. Remember, for appetizers and salad, start on the outside and work your way in.

For life's main course, work your way from the inside out.

Adornment

WEAR THE COLORS OF WHERE YOU ARE and how your life unfolds. Do not be ashamed of a tattered beginning, of jeans frayed by ventures into unexplored territory. These will shield you from the cold wind in the same way as do the others' silk scarves and fine linen.

If you would try on different clothing, then picture yourself wearing a different life.

Imagine changing your outfit—starting with your socks and underwear. Refuse to accept that you are not meant to shop in the upscale boutique if that's what you want.

And, really, if you like sitting around in your pajamas all day, then stop apologizing for it. No one's going to shoot you for it. Holy underwear is no less blessed.

Find what feels good.

Never deny your self as there is nothing worth caring for more. But do it because you love the gift of wrinkled flesh and tired knees, not because you might fall down and want to measure up should another opt to help you up.

Worn shoes will take you where you need to go.

Changing Clothes

Or you might decide to change your clothes.

If you desire, you can try on a different life for size.

In the world you live in now, it is customary to accept so much as fixed and unchangeable: your family, your name, your home, your chosen profession.

Choice is your birthright.

If you long to plow the field, try on a pair of overalls for size. If you want to experience the explorer's grand adventures, pick up the binoculars and see.

This is more than dressing the part.

It is stepping into the role and opening yourself to the experience with the belief that you may become what you choose to become.

Leaving Limitation Behind

TO MOVE FORWARD AND BEYOND the restricted life, you must cut loose the ropes with which you bind yourself. Refuse to limit yourself to the designated field to which others might confine you and to which you yourself see as the boundary of your experience.

This does not mean you must leave a particular field of experience. If you are content to run the bases, run them well.

If you long to play a different sport, find your team.

Scope out the best location. Gather the equipment you will need. Study those who have done it best, and embrace the love of the game.

If you don't feel called out onto the playing field, walk on. Find the experience that brings out the best in you.

Love your life. Empty it of every thought that tells you why you can't.

Snack Time

SAVOR THE DELIGHTS OF DOING NOTHING and then seeing everything come clear. Watch the bliss bubble up like laughter in the glass from which you drink your life.

Feel the warmth of the ale and the wide-awake feeling of the snowflake that settles on your cheek like a fresh kiss. Listen to the songbirds and the coyote's howl. Hear the distinct growl of traffic.

Feel the turning of the day to night.

Whatever course you choose for your life, give yourself time to dawdle. Go fishing.

Stand in the stream and see how far you've come.

Catch the fish and let him go. Look down river at the stones settled here. See the water pooling, then finding once again its way in the direction of its home, moving from source to source, rising up and falling down, becoming again and again.

Form and Function

YOU FEAR CHANGING FORM, for you define your self by the state of your being. You are so much more.

You are not confined by the shape of your body or its covering. You are not reduced to the accessorized life.

Neither are you made invisible simply because you shift into spirit.

And when you fall softly to the ground and flow again into liquid possibility, the flow in which you find yourself is not mere necessity of transportation from one place to the next.

Form can follow function. Or form can simply be form—not the total definition of who you are.

What is most important to you at a point in time may lead to a choice about the form you choose to take. Again, the function you choose to fill or follow is not meant to be your final destination.

Find your way through form and function.

Fly unencumbered by thoughts that tether your circumference or bind you to a field of being fixed by false center point.

Become a Connoisseur of Change

TASTE TIME. Sip it like fine wine. Raise your glass and toast this life. Drink it up, and then move on to another day, another tasting.

Savor the moments. Especially those that don't go as you had planned.

Try something new on the menu when you have the opportunity. When life serves up the same old same old, give thanks. And look for opportunities on life's ever-changing menu. Say yes to a new variety of experience that can open you up to the flow of good.

Take the long way home. Have breakfast for supper. Eat dessert first.

Set off on an adventure without a full itinerary. Look for someone new to meet today, and discover something new about your self.

Change it up and watch what happens next.

Never Miss an Opportunity to Choose

CHOICE IS A SACRED GIFT.

See all your choices like candy lined up before you—every piece of it delicious.

Let your mouth water at the options and then go ahead; pick your favorite color—the one that is calling out, "Choose me! Choose me!" And if you have no clear favorite, close your eyes and point your fingers and say "Yes" to what says yes to you.

Even if the decision that is before you seems serious and a painful choice between two lesser ways, see the very opportunity to choose as a divinely given moment to express your creative being and contribute to the unfolding of life and all that is.

You are loved no matter what consequence follows your choice.
You are treasured regardless of the result you co-create.

You are cherished in the choosing, bathed in the blessed assurance of having the gift of choice.

Stand Your Ground

YOU FEEL AS IF YOU ARE WAKING from a long midsummer night's dream, but just as quickly decide the new spiritual reality coming into focus is, in fact, the dream.

When others insist that you are only dreaming of a more fanciful version of the facts, you relinquish your tentative hold on a truth you have barely begun to recover.

When they say you have been mistaken in believing that you and they are great spirits unbound by time, you succumb and are coaxed back into the alluring half-wakened state that many of you reading are actually in.

When you are told that you are losing your grip on reality, stand your ground.

When someone says your head is in the clouds, remind yourself that your heart beats from the river of life. Smile at your friend and be grateful for the gift of imagination—and for your spirit free and unencumbered by what you once saw as present reality.

So, live the dream, and hold fast to the truth of who you are.

Free Spirit

THE BIG IDEA IS THIS: you are bound only by your reluctance to allow your heart to beat in its natural rhythm with all of life, born of Spirit.

You are restricted only when you fail to realign your growth in the natural direction of the Source of your very breath. Unbind yourselves from all that would tether your great spirit to a set of rules or to a perspective formed from a single vantage point.

You are free to sample. You are free to choose.

Yet, when you climb back into the same small box again and again because you have been told that that is where you belong or because you were born into one tradition or another and have been told you must live in a certain way, eventually you come to believe that the box is the world.

Or worse, you become consumed by a crippling fear that the great unknown beyond the constricting circumference of that beautiful box are the badlands, filled with danger. You begin to believe that, should you venture outside of your designated air space, you will be shot down and fall into forgetfulness.

You begin to believe that the air inside the box is the source of your life, your sustenance—all that keeps you alive.

But a box, even an ornate treasure box—no matter how beautiful—is, in the end, a box.

If you love one present you have opened here, if it brings you comfort and joy and becomes a special place for you to be fully you, then by all means return again and again. Just don't forget that the world is round, not square. It is a tiny blue dot brimming with beautiful boxes of every variety.

Above all, know that you are created free, apart from fear,
sealed in a timeless love unbroken by the human condition.

Some have called it a love that will not let you go. Even if you have let it go and fixed yourself to a particular expression of that love, you are held safe and protected. The darkness that you imagine beyond can never extinguish your bright light.

Intrepid Souls in Transit

YOU LEARN AS CHILDREN of the great explorers and wish you could explore new lands or sail upon the seas in search of all that is yet to be discovered.

You can. You do. You are radiant and resplendent.
You are restless, ready for life's grand adventure.

You're off! And still you stand on life's deck, looking around, confused. Are you waiting for permission to pull up the anchor and set sail? Puzzled by the unfamiliar bay in which you find yourselves, many of you choose to treat this life as if it were some shore leave.

Life is the adventure, my friends!
Now is your voyage of discovery.

Your very soul is the compass that will always lead you home. And if ever you feel uncertain, let the light of the stars lead you on. The story of your adventure on the high seas of this world will live on.

But first you have to risk the journey.

Pirates!

MOVE THROUGH LIFE WITH HONOR, but don't forfeit your sense of play just because someone else would judge you or label you a miscreant. Know who you are and hold life and love sacred. Awaken to the thrill of another day on the high seas of life.

Enjoy the adventure!

There may be an occasion in which you have been the hero but are not recognized as such. Let it be what it is and move on. Swashbuckle your way if you must, but refuse to abandon your principles or your sense of style.

Live with a sense of gratitude for what provisions you share, and celebrate life's journey.

Goodbyes

CHOOSING WHEN TO STAY and when to go seems sometimes the hardest choice of all. But in your choice to say goodbye, know you greet the moment again and again.

When I have gone, you may well remember me.

Or in sweet forgetfulness imagine someone other than who I was. You may re-experience the first kiss or savor the memory of our last dance.

Meet me in a field. Dare the rapids with me in a dream.
Carry me, and I will carry you.

P.S.

THE END is always the beginning.

Begin.
And begin again.

Books by This Author
Visit DawnRicherson.com/books

Cultivating Essence from the Matrix of Soul
Awakening the World Within
Finding Our Forward Flow
Embracing a New Vision
Seeds for Life

All Systems Go

Birds of a Feather
True Identity
A Reconciliation of Light
12 Doors of Abundance

Energetic Perspectives

Journey to the Heartland
Journey to Sacred Wholeness
Sacred Partnership

Many Rivers Flow
Across the Seas of Time
Testament: A Half-Life in Poems
The Magda Poems

From the Heart of a Child
To Sin by Silence

www.ingramcontent.com/pod-product-compliance
Lightning Source LLC
Chambersburg PA
CBHW061203010526
44110CB00064B/2666